PLYMOUTH

A shortish guide

Robert Hesketh

Bossiney Books

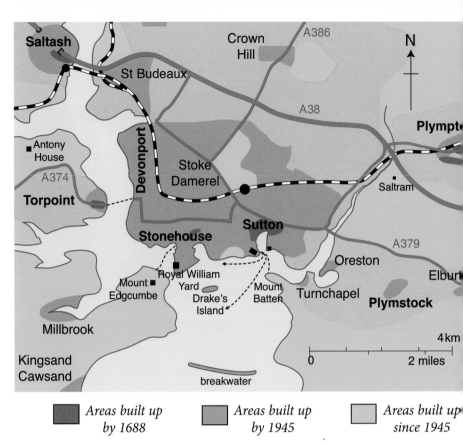

| Areas built up by 1688 | Areas built up by 1945 | Areas built up since 1945 |

The growth of Plymouth as a conurbation, showing the areas built up at different periods

Acknowledgements
The maps are by Nick Hawken. The cover is based on a design by Heards Design Partnership. All photographs are by the author or from the publishers' own collection.

First published 2010 by Bossiney Books Ltd
Langore, Launceston, Cornwall PL15 8LD
www.bossineybooks.com
ISBN 978-1-906474-28-7
Printed in Great Britain by R Booth Ltd, Penryn, Cornwall

INTRODUCTION

Plymouth's ancient quays and narrow cobbled streets recall its long history and contrast strikingly with both the post-war reconstruction and the bold modern architecture of the city centre.

The Sound is a superb natural harbour and the city's destiny has always been tied to the sea. The Sound is also one of the finest settings enjoyed by any British city, whether seen from the Hoe or from one of the delightful boat trips from the Barbican.

As both a fishing and a trading port from its earliest days, Plymouth played a sizeable role in overseas settlement – most famously the *Mayflower*, bound for America, sailed from here, as did the earliest settler ships to Australia and New Zealand. The city's name is also linked to exploration; Captain Cook started all his voyages of discovery from Plymouth and Charles Darwin began his voyage in the *Beagle* from Devonport.

Above all, Plymouth has been the keystone to the nation's naval defence. Guarding the Western Approaches to the Channel, the city grew as Britain's western bastion against invasion and blockade. Drake sailing from Plymouth to repel the Spanish Armada has become part of the national legend, but the city's role in defeating Napoleon's navy and defending Britain's Atlantic supply lifeline through two world wars was no less crucial.

Above: Plympton St Maurice, which had a Norman castle and a priory: substantial remains of the castle survive

Below: The 'Prysten House' in Plymouth is so called because it was previously thought to have housed the priests of St Andrews. In fact it was built by Thomas Yogge, a rich merchant.

Bordeaux wine, Devon cloth and fish were among the chief goods traded at Plymouth. Provisioning, accommodating and transporting pilgrims – inward to Canterbury and outward to Santiago de Compostela in Spain – was also profitable

HISTORY

The Medieval period

Plymouth was of no great size or significance before the 13th century. There had been a Bronze Age camp at Sutton Pool and a small trading settlement at Mount Batten from 1000 BC to the end of the Roman era. However, what was to become the nucleus of Plymouth was for centuries merely a small farming and fishing settlement known as Sutton (Old English for 'South Farm') by the present Sutton Harbour. In time, Sutton eclipsed neighbouring Plympton which, with its Norman castle and priory, was initially larger and richer.

At high tide the Plym reached medieval Plympton, then a port and one of only four Devon Stannary towns handling Dartmoor tin.

However, tin streaming on Dartmoor created silt and waste which washed down its rivers, clogging them (especially the Plym) and making them hard for ships to navigate. At the mouth of the Plym, Sutton had all the facilities ships' masters needed: deep water and shelter as well as victuallers, sailmakers and carpenters – and, no doubt, ale houses and pretty Devon maids too.

'Plymouth' was first recorded as such in 1211, at which time Dartmouth and Fowey were bigger ports and Saltash controlled the river Tamar's mouth. Plymouth's early growth owed much to the lucrative wine trade with Bordeaux. It was granted a market in 1254, thus making it a town – though it was officially 'Sutton Prior' as the Prior of Plympton controlled the market rights.

A fleet of warships assembled in Plymouth in 1294. It was the first of many war fleets. In time, Plymouth outstripped Dartmouth and Fowey and became England's chief naval base on the western Channel coast. Although both these western ports could offer shelter as good as or better than Plymouth's, they suffered the disadvantages of narrow harbour entrances and difficult land access.

Unfortunately, any naval centre where men and ships gather, supplies are handled and ships built, invites enemy attack. Plymouth was repeatedly attacked during the Hundred Years War with France (1373-1453), most notoriously in 1403 when a large Breton force ravaged and burnt part of the town outside Martyn's Gate. This has been called Bretonside ever since. After this raid, Plymouth's defences were improved with a castle and a wall, which gained the four gates that still appear on the city's Coat of Arms. These defences were later extended with bulwarks and gun platforms on the Hoe in the 16th century – the remains can be seen beneath Hoe Road. The Citadel (page 26), ordered in 1666 at around the same time as the Mount Batten Tower (page 30), marked a further development in Plymouth's defences.

Despite brief halts caused by war, trade multiplied. Medieval Plymouth expanded – Plymouth Gin's Distillery (page 22) is a notable survivor with early 15th century origins, whilst the Prysten House is slightly later, c1498.

Meanwhile, Plymouth grew in political importance. In 1298 the town sent burgesses to Parliament for the first time. The first reference to Plymouth's Mayor was in 1369. In 1440, Plymouth gained borough status and was the first town in England incorporated by Act of Parliament.

A house in the High Street of Sutton Prior, now Buckwell Street (left) and the Merchant's House in St Andrew Street, both sixteenth century

Plymouth in the 16th century

Medieval Plymouth was bound to the sea, but in trade and war it was involved only with Europe. The 16th century brought a new era of worldwide exploration and settlement, in which Plymouth and its most famous citizen, Sir Francis Drake, played a leading role.

Between 1532 and 1600 Plymouth doubled in size and overtook Dartmouth as Devon's leading naval port. Plymouth's maritime trade developed too, led by the expanding Newfoundland cod fishery which was a great training ground for sailors and ships. The old order was changing: Plymouth was relieved of its annual payment to Plympton Priory in 1534 and lost its religious houses, the Greyfriars and the Whitefriars, in 1538 during King Henry VIII's break with the Catholic Church and Dissolution of England's monasteries.

Buckland Abbey was sold to Drake by the younger Sir Richard Grenville, one of Elizabethan Devon's boldest sailors and adventurers, later celebrated by Tennyson in his poem 'The Revenge'

Plympton Priory became a quarry, whilst Buckland Abbey (page 37), 13km north of Plymouth, was bought by Sir Richard Grenville who began converting it into the Tudor mansion visitors see today. His famous grandson (also Sir Richard) sold Buckland to Sir Francis Drake in 1581.

Drake was born 6km from Buckland Abbey, at Crowndale, around 1541. He first gained fame with his West Indian and Pacific voyages. Setting sail again from Plymouth in 1577, Drake entered the Pacific and plundered his way northwards as far as what is now British Columbia. By the time he reached Drake's Bay (San Francisco), he had lost all his five ships except the *Golden Hind* – but had a stupendous haul of looted treasure. The safest way home was the boldest – to avoid the hated Spanish and sail westwards across the Pacific. After three years at sea, Drake dropped anchor in Plymouth Sound in 1580 and received a hero's welcome.

In 1581, Queen Elizabeth I knighted Drake aboard the *Golden Hind*. He became MP and Mayor of Plymouth and was instrumental in building 'Drake's Leat', purportedly to supply Plymouth with water, but cleverly manipulated for his own profit.

Drake and Plymouth are rightly remembered above all for the defeat of the Spanish Armada in 1588. Spain had assembled the largest war fleet ever seen with the aim of invading England, dethroning Elizabeth and forcing the country back to Catholicism. England's western forces were concentrated in Plymouth, with more than sixty ships anchored in the Hamoaze and Cattewater.

It would seem there was not a moment to lose in attacking when the Armada was sighted on 19 July, but Sir Francis Drake, showing suitable contempt for the enemy, is said to have coolly insisted on finishing his game of bowls on Plymouth Hoe before weighing anchor. Although some have scoffed at this story, Drake was undoubtedly well aware that strong south-westerly winds had bottled up the English ships at Plymouth and the only way to get them out to sea was on a strong ebb tide. That day, high tide was 10.31 pm. When the Armada was sighted and Drake informed, it would therefore have been either dead low water or a rising tide.

Once at sea, Drake took a leading part in harrying the Spanish fleet with hit and run attacks and fire ships, driving the unwieldy galleons up the Channel and so into the North Sea, where they had no hope of the planned rendezvous with Spanish forces in the Netherlands. Foul weather in northern waters hastened the Armada's further disintegration and destruction, as the Spaniards attempted to sail around Scotland and home.

Drake's statue on the Hoe.

In highlighting Drake, we should not forget his cousin, John Hawkins.

Another Plymothian, Hawkins was knighted for his part in defeating the Armada. Made Treasurer of the Navy in 1578 and Comptroller in 1589, Hawkins had a distinguished career which, like Drake's, included being a Plymouth MP. Both men met their deaths attacking the Spanish in the Caribbean 1595-96.

Much less creditably, Hawkins is also remembered as the first of many Englishmen to trade in African slaves. He was so far from being ashamed of this that he had an African in chains on his crest

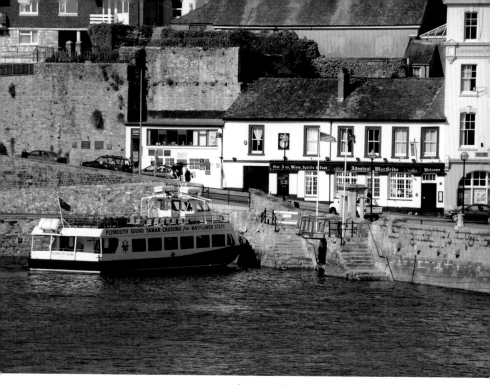

The Mayflower Steps at high tide

The Mayflower

The *Mayflower* sailed from Plymouth for Virginia with 102 passengers plus crew in September 1620. 'Separatists', who refused to conform to the worship prescribed by the Church of England, they undertook the hazardous transatlantic voyage seeking a new life of religious freedom in America. Later known as 'Pilgrims', their story of triumph over danger and hardship has a leading role in America's popular culture and national mythology, as well as strengthening the sense of shared destiny between Britain and the United States.

Initially, there were two Pilgrim vessels. The *Speedwell* carried English Separatists who had first settled in Protestant Holland, where they had found religious toleration but an alien culture and language. *Speedwell* joined the *Mayflower* and her English passengers at Southampton in August 1620, but she developed a leak and the two ships put in at Dartmouth for refitting. Sailing from there, *Speedwell* again leaked and the Pilgrims turned back to Plymouth – some believing *Speedwell's* crew had sabotaged her to escape the hazards of the voyage.

Thus the *Mayflower* sailed alone from Plymouth and the Pilgrims later named their settlement in Massachusetts 'Plymouth'.

Probably Plymouth, Devon, had welcomed them. Many Puritans lived in Plymouth, which largely determined the town's allegiance to Parliament when Civil War came in 1642, with its strong element of religious conflict. Plymouth distinguished itself throughout the war during a harsh and prolonged siege and never surrendered.

Bound for 'North Virginia' – an area near the Hudson River – the *Mayflower* was blown off course and landed in Cape Cod after 66 gruelling days at sea. She was a grossly overcrowded vessel of a mere 180 tons. Only half the Pilgrim party and *Mayflower's* crew survived the first freezing winter in New England, where an outbreak of disease was made worse by poor diet.

However, they stayed and Plymouth remains the oldest permanent European settlement in the United States – a fact celebrated in Plymouth Massachusetts with museums, a recreated 1627 village and more besides. The Thanksgiving feast the survivors held in 1621 developed into an annual tradition in America, with powerful patriotic as well as religious associations.

Other famous voyages

Ships carrying settlers and explorers have sailed from Plymouth to all corners of the globe. Several are celebrated on plaques around Mayflower Steps and next to the Barbican's Admiral MacBride pub.

They span a wide period. Whilst one celebrates the first transatlantic flight in 1919 by the American seaplane NC4, another commemorates Sir Humphrey Gilbert, who sailed from Plymouth in 1583 and claimed Newfoundland for Queen Elizabeth – overlooking the fact that Europeans from several nations (England included) had been fishing the Grand Banks for nearly a century before. And of course Native Americans were not consulted about Newfoundland, nor about Virginia, claimed for Elizabeth by Philip Amadas and Ralph Barlow, sent from Plymouth in 1584 by Sir Walter Raleigh, patron of the abortive Roanoke Colony (1587-90).

Sea Venture sailed from Plymouth in 1609 with settlers and supplies for the infant Jamestown colony in Virginia. Like the *Mayflower* they missed their mark in a storm and landed on uninhabited Bermuda, thus beginning its history as a British colony. It is thought their story inspired Shakespeare's play *The Tempest*.

Captain James Cook (1728-79) began all three of his great voyages of discovery from Plymouth

In 1787 the transport ships *Friendship* and *Charlotte* sailed for Australia with a cargo of convicts in 'the First Fleet'. With nine other transport ships they landed at Port Jackson, which became Sydney.

Another plaque commemorates Plymouth men who helped found modern Australia, including Tobias Furneaux who charted the coast of Tasmania and Cornishman Captain William Bligh, who survived mutiny aboard the *Bounty* to become Governor of New South Wales. Both accompanied Cook on his second voyage from Plymouth.

White Australia was largely founded on convict labour. A plaque near Mayflower Steps recalls four 'Tolpuddle Martyrs' who landed in Plymouth in 1838 after being transported to Australia. Their 'crime' had been swearing a secret oath as members of the Friendly Society of Agricultural Labourers.

Tory, the pioneer ship in the colonisation of New Zealand, sailed from Plymouth in 1839. Another plaque commemorates six Plymouth Company vessels carrying West Country settlers to New Plymouth, New Zealand between 1840 and 1842.

Charles Darwin was just 22 when he sailed aboard the *Beagle* from Devonport in 1831 as a gentleman naturalist. However, his observations during the five-year-long round-the-world voyage and his reflections upon them led to *The Origin of Species* (published 1859), a book which set in train revolutionary changes in science and thought on humankind which still reverberate today.

Captain Robert Falcon Scott (1868-1912) is commemorated with a memorial on Mount Wise. Born in Plymouth (Stoke Damerel), Scott led two Antarctic expeditions – the second cost his life and those of his companions.

The Devonport naval dockyard in 2010

The French Wars and the growth of 'Dock'

By 1800 a quarter of Britain's state expenditure went to the Royal Navy. A good proportion of that was spent on Dock (Devonport), which played a crucial role as Britain's leading western port, building and supplying warships and stationing men and materials. Ships sailed from Plymouth Sound to fight all over the world, blockade France, deter invasion and guard the Western Approaches.

Dock's trade was war: Britain was at war with France for 67 out of the 127 years between 1689 and the end of the Napoleonic Wars in 1815. The growth of Dock was integral to the development of the British Empire and the emergence of Britain as the world's leading naval power.

Known as Devonport after 1824, Dock was chosen in 1690 in preference to Turnchapel (page 30), Torbay, Bideford, Exmouth and Dartmouth, as Britain's warlike response to France's new naval yards in Brest, ordered by Louis XIV in 1688. A modern stone-built naval yard, Dock had one wet and two dry docks for first rate ships and enough stores to supply forty ships of the line.

Dock and Plymouth too benefited from the Eddystone Lighthouse. The first lighthouse was built in 1696 and lost in the Great Storm of 1703. A second lighthouse was burned down in 1755. Today, the third Eddystone Lighthouse, known as 'Smeaton's Tower', stands on Plymouth Hoe (page 24). The fourth, built in 1882, still stands sentinel 14km beyond Rame Head, guiding ships away from the dangerous Eddystone Rocks towards the safety of Plymouth Sound.

The dockyards were expanded in 1727 to cover 54 acres. New houses sprang up – many built with wood granted by (or pilfered from) the dockyards. Dock had a population of 3000 by 1733, rising to 12,000 in 1780 and 24,000 during the Napoleonic Wars.

During the Seven Years War (1756-63), the dockyards were further extended and formidable new defences and barracks built to protect Dock and the new Royal Naval Hospital, Stonehouse. The American War of Independence (1776-83), followed by war with Revolutionary and then Napoleonic France from 1793 to 1815, brought further expansions to the dockyards and defences.

It also brought many French prisoners of war. They were initially housed in hulks – old ships moored in Plymouth Sound. Eventually, there were more prisoners than the hulks could hold and a new prison was built at Princetown on Dartmoor. The first party of prisoners arrived from Plymouth under armed guard in 1809. They were joined by American POWs in 1812. Dartmoor prison began taking civilian convicts from 1850.

Plymouth Breakwater, the largest and most expensive single development, was begun in 1812. It took 32 years to complete and cost the then colossal sum of £1 million, but was so well built with 3^1/$_2$ million tons of stone that it continues to protect Plymouth Sound from southerly storms, a vital task, while its lighthouse guides ships into safe channels.

Plymouth Breakwater can be seen behind the warship

The Royal William Yard was closed in 1992.

It has since been redeveloped with luxury apartments, shops, restaurants and art galleries

Post 1815 developments

Peace in 1815 brought depression to Plymouth. Suddenly, there were no enemy prize ships with valuable cargoes to enrich the town. The Navy discharged six sailors out of every seven. Plymouth had 7000 paupers and the Hoe Road was started in 1818 to supplement the Breakwater in providing work.

The new Custom House (page 22) was built in 1820, followed by a much larger project, the Royal William Victualling Yard (page 34). Designed by Sir John Rennie and built between 1824 and 1835, the site covers 6ha and had depots for food, rum and equipment, a slaughterhouse and repair workshops. It is named after King William IV, who had been a naval officer and often visited Plymouth before becoming king (1830-37). His statue stands over the entrance gate.

Meanwhile, the Steam Age came to Devonport, which completed its first steamship in 1832. A new steam yard, with basins, docks and a steam factory, was built at Keyham between 1844 and 1854.

In the 1860s, renewed fear of war with France led Palmerston's government to build a ring of 29 forts and interlocking batteries around Plymouth and Devonport to prevent attack from sea or land. Completed by 1870 as part of a large national naval defence pro-gramme, they were known as 'Palmerston's Follies' because war with France never came. One of them, Crownhill Fort, has been restored and is occasionally open to the public (01752 793754). It has seven bastions and was used as a barracks until the 1980s, but preserves the original buildings inside.

Meanwhile, the fleet was outgrowing Devonport. The 54 hectare

Devonport's Grecian town hall, and the neighbouring Egyptian building, were originally part of a larger group of imposing buildings, including a 'Hindoo' temple, and have not always been as much cherished as they should have been

extension at Keyham, built between 1895 and 1907 with huge new docks and basins, nearly doubled the dockyard area. This was matched by new naval barracks, completed in 1903.

Defence spending helped drive Plymouth's growth. In 1815, the combined population of Plymouth, Stonehouse and Devonport was 56,000. When the three towns were formally united in 1914, this had risen to 209,000. During that period, the Royal Dockyards launched 170 ships and by 1912 over 12,000 people were employed.

Plymouth was one of Victorian Britain's most densely populated cities. Immigrants poured into the city looking for work in the dockyards or in the expanding civilian industries, including building, chemicals and quarrying. Many came from Cornwall and Devon, especially when mining had one of its many downturns. Others came on cheap passages from Ireland: only Liverpool had a bigger Irish population than Plymouth, according to the 1861 census.

As well as overcrowded slums, Plymouth gained from Britain's rapid industrialisation, notably the mainline railway from London in 1848 and a place on the steamship map of the world in 1850 when a new dock was built for the Cape Mails.

There were grand civic developments too. One of the best examples is Devonport's imposing town hall in Ker Street, designed like a Greek temple by John Foulston and built in 1821. Foulston also built Ker Street's Institution in Egyptian style two years later.

Dignified terraces of spacious houses were built for the well-to-do. Some of the most attractive overlook the sea, including the Esplanade and Elliot Terrace on the Hoe. Beneath the Hoe are further fine examples, such as Great Western Road and Eddystone Terrace.

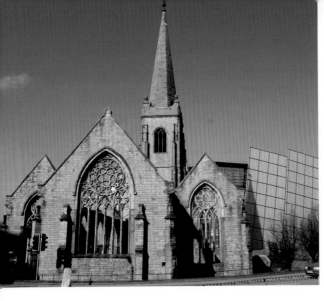

Charles Church, deliberately preserved in ruins as a memorial of the Blitz and Plymouth's Second World War civilian casualties: 1172 killed and 3269 seriously injured

1939-45 Destruction and idealistic rebuild

A prime military target, much of old Plymouth was destroyed between 1940 and 1944. For its size, it was Britain's most heavily bombed city. The Luftwaffe dropped 1228 tons of explosives in 59 raids on Plymouth, killing 1172 civilians, destroying 3700 houses and damaging 72,000 more. Servicemen returning from abroad found it hard to recognise the gutted city centre.

The *Plan for Plymouth* was published in 1943. Brainchild of City Engineer James Paton Watson, renowned architect Professor Patrick Abercrombie and Lord Astor, the Lord Mayor, its vision was not only to rebuild Plymouth, but to free the city from overcrowded slums and traffic congestion caused by narrow, horse-age streets.

Housing was top priority. A crash programme saw the thousandth pre-fabricated home built in 1946. Large council house estates grew up in the fields around the old city. Between 1951 and 1957 over a thousand permanent council houses were built each year. Supplemented by large scale private and MOD developments, the new estates offered a more spacious life centred on their own shops, schools, parks and facilities.

The brave new world of the housing estates was matched by a transformed city centre. Only a few buildings had survived the bombs in central Plymouth. They and the old tangled street pattern were swept away. In their place rose a bold grid pattern of broad streets lined with angular modern buildings like an American city.

Armada Way, with its vista of the Hoe and its Naval Memorial, forms the north/south axis of the new city centre. It crosses the east/west axis, Royal Parade, with its large department stores, by the Guildhall (page 27). An inner ring road encloses the central shopping district, which is kept only for local traffic.

Begun in 1947, at a time of great austerity, the new city centre was largely complete by 1955. With a few modifications, including more pedestrianised streets and shopping malls, it has remained true to the original vision of its planners.

Since 1945

Balancing old and new, progress with preservation, modern city centre with historic Barbican, has been the theme of post-war Plymouth. That Plymouth's history and heritage draws increasing numbers of visitors is in good part thanks to the Plymouth Barbican Association, founded to preserve the best of Plymouth's oldest quarter amid the rush to rebuild the city and clear its slums after the Second World War. Happily, they have succeeded in preserving the Barbican's character and refurbishing many historic buildings in Britain's greatest area of cobbled streets.

'Plymouth is enjoying prosperity unknown in her long history,' boasted the Chamber of Commerce in 1961. By then, Plymouth had its new city centre, huge areas of new housing and many new factories. Also new were the Tamar road bridge (page 36), Laira Bridge and the Civic Centre (page 27); whilst the Guildhall and St Andrew's church (page 27) had been restored.

Plymouth's boundaries were expanded in 1949 to include the new housing estates and again in 1967 to include Plympton and Plymstock. Plymouth expanded as an educational centre too.

The Polytechnic was launched in 1965 and became the University of Plymouth in 1992. It is now (2010) the largest university in the

South-West with over 30,000 students and is one of the campuses for the Peninsula Medical School, established in 2000. St Mark and St John, a teacher training college, moved to Plymouth in 1973 from Chelsea. The National Marine Aquarium, a superb educational facility (page 35), was opened in 1998.

The city has also developed as a yachting centre, with four sizeable modern marinas. Sutton Harbour and Queen Anne's Battery Marinas complement the Barbican. Plymouth Yacht Haven lies just across the water at Turnchapel (page 30), whilst Mayflower International Marina is opposite the Royal William Yard (page 34) at Mount Wise.

Despite the growth in tourism and service industries, Plymouth is still an industrial and above all a naval centre. Inevitably, the 1945 peak of over 17,000 dockyard jobs declined but the dockyards were kept busy long after the war with a series of major re-fitting contracts, whilst new factories producing everything from chewing gum to electronics meant new jobs.

Despite many changes in the armed forces, a series of developments kept defence money flowing into the city. Notably, Plymouth became the Royal Marine Commando base in 1973 and a nuclear submarine base was built at Keyham in 1978, along with a massive frigate re-fit complex just north of the Torpoint ferry.

The end of the Cold War and the post-2007 recession makes the dockyard's future uncertain, but at the time of writing it constitutes the largest naval base in western Europe, extending over 5km (3 miles) of waterfront. The dockyard and the armed forces remain crucial to Plymouth's economy.

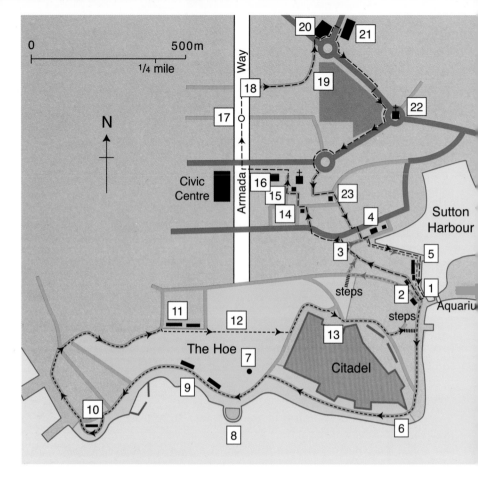

THREE SHORT TRAILS

The Barbican Trail

Start from the Mayflower Steps, on the western side of the lock gates of Sutton Harbour. Many voyages have begun and ended from Sutton Harbour, as a series of plaques by the Steps recall (see pages 10-11). Today, the pier near the Steps is the departure point for ferries to Mount Batten, Cawsand and the Royal William Yard, as well as sight-seeing and fishing trips.

Walk inland past the Tourist Information Centre and Plymouth Mayflower (1) and after another 50m turn left at Island House, which bears the names of the pilgrims who sailed from the Barbican in 1620. Continue gently uphill into cobbled NEW STREET to visit the Elizabethan House (2).

The Elizabethan House

One of several timber-fronted 16th and 17th century merchants' houses in New Street, it is open to the public (entry fee) and gives a vivid impression of daily life in Elizabeth's reign. It was first recorded in 1584 and its furniture and fittings are of that time. The kitchen has an open fireplace with spit roasts, an oak settle and iron cooking pots. Steps lead up to a kitchen garden. Mount the pole staircase (built around a ship's mast) to the parlour, with its leaded windows and sloping floors.

Plymouth Mayflower

Plymouth Mayflower tells the city's story, especially its naval history, with audio visual displays, exhibits and tableaux. Work your way down through the centuries from the top floor (which has a magnificent view of Sutton Harbour) through Drake and the Pilgrim Fathers to modern times on the first floor.

Continue up New Street past the Elizabethan Garden. Turn right opposite the Garrison Steps into FRIARS LANE. Turn left into SOUTHSIDE STREET, passing on your right a mural by eccentric Plymouth artist Robert Lenkiewicz (1941-2002) above a small shopping arcade with jewellery and art shops. You will then come to the Plymouth Gin Distillery (3). Walk through the narrow alley opposite the Distillery, BLACKFRIARS OPE.

At the end of the alley turn right along the cobbled street. On the right is the Old Custom House, on the left the New Custom House (4), built in 1810 and still in use.

Plymouth Gin Distillery
Guided tours explain the history of Plymouth Gin and how it is made – though the exact recipe is kept secret. The building is thought to be early 15th century and to have begun as a refectory for local friars. It became a distillery in 1793 and is the only place where Plymouth Gin is made. Downstairs is a gin shop, upstairs a bar and brasserie with a medieval timber roof.

The view from the top floor of the Plymouth Mayflower

The New Custom House (left) and the Three Crowns, one of a number of estab-lishments catering for outdoor eating

Next door is the Three Crowns with tables overlooking Sutton Pool. Keep right and follow the south side of Sutton Pool, where many of the tall warehouses have been converted to pubs and restaurants, to the former Fish Market (5). A clothes and gift store at the time of writing, if it looks rather like a Victorian railway station, that's because it was designed in 1896 by the GWR's Engineer, Sir James Inglis. Continue along the Quay behind it, back to the Mayflower Steps.

The Hoe Trail

From the Mayflower Steps, head seaward (THE HOE AND WATERFRONT). Walk uphill past the 'Admiral MacBride' – as MP for Plymouth 1784-1790 MacBride got the grants for building the Barbican piers. Just beyond the pub are a series of plaques commemorating Plymouth's historic maritime connections (see pages 10-11).

Smeaton's Tower

There are great 360 degree views from the balcony of Smeaton's Tower (limited opening year round, fee) over the city, Drake's Island, the Breakwater and the Citadel. Built in 1756-59, the tower originally stood as a lighthouse on the Eddystone Reef, 14km south of Plymouth. When the rock it stood on was eroded, Smeaton's Tower was moved block by dovetailed block to the Hoe and re-erected between 1882-84. An image of Smeaton's Tower appeared with Britannia on penny coins for many years up to 1970. Plaques explain the tower's history and the simple furniture of the bedroom, kitchen and oil room you pass through as you climb to the lantern.

Right: The restored Tinside Pool

Below: The Hoe terraces, seen from the Sound

Continue along Madeira Road and follow it right by a pair of ship's cannon (6). Enjoy the view east to Mount Batten, the Cattewater and Turnchapel and south to Plymouth Breakwater (page 13). Follow the waterfront with the Citadel to your right. Keep left at the roundabout by Smeaton's Tower (7). Just down the hill is Tinside Lido (8). First opened in 1935, this art deco swimming pool (Grade II listed) has been refurbished. Follow Hoe Road past the tiered Belvedere of 1891 (9) into Grand Parade. Take the footpath to the left around Eddystone Terrace (10) for a good view of the Hoe and Drake Island (page 31).

Continue left into Great Western Road. Bear left then immediately turn right into CLIFF ROAD and follow it steadily uphill to the Hoe.

The Citadel gateway, decorated with Charles II's coat of arms. Charles ordered the Citadel to update Plymouth's defences during war with the Dutch in 1666. Defending Sutton Harbour in combination with artillery on Mount Batten, the Citadel's guns also faced inland.

This protected it from attack from the rear, but it may also have been intended to intimidate Plymouth, a staunchly Puritan city which had held out for Parliament against King Charles I during the English Civil War (1642-46), despite a prolonged siege.

Follow the tarmac Promenade towards Smeaton's Tower.

On the left is Elliot Terrace (11), built by John Pethick, who also designed the Guildhall (page 27). Viscount and Lady Astor, who were Lord Mayor and Lady Mayoress during World War Two, lived at number 3. Lady Nancy Astor was also Britain's first woman MP. A native of Virginia, she represented Plymouth Sutton from 1919 to 1945.

Sir Francis Drake's statue (12) was erected in 1884 at the zenith of British imperialism. The Armada Memorial followed in 1888. Between them stands Plymouth Naval Memorial commemorating 7251 sailors of the First World War and 15,933 of the Second World War.

Continue to the far end of the Promenade and turn left on the path above West Hoe Road. Follow the path when it bends sharp right, then descend steps. When the road bends left, continue ahead past the Citadel's main gateway (13).

From the Citadel gateway, continue ahead BARBICAN SEA FRONT and down LAMBHAY HILL. Bear left down a dead end street past the Commercial Inn, then descend the steps back to the Barbican.

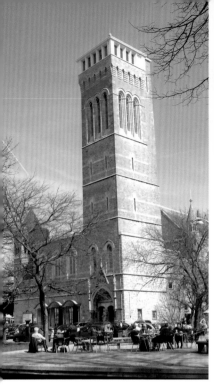

Above: Opposite the Guildhall, and in contrast to it, is the Civic Centre (17), built in 1961

Left: The Guildhall, dating from 1870, was largely rebuilt after wartime damage. The windows in the main hall show scenes from Plymouth's history

City Centre Trail

From the Mayflower Steps, turn inland and walk past Island House on your left into Southside Street. Look above street level to see good 17th and 18th century frontages. Continue past several interesting galleries and the Plymouth Gin Distillery (page 22).

At the end of Southside Street, turn left into Vauxhall Street, CITY CENTRE MERCHANT'S HOUSE. Cross the street and turn first right. The Merchant's House is 100m ahead. Turn left along the cobbled alley above the Merchant's House (14). Turn right to see Prysten House (15). Wrongly thought to have been the priests' ('Prysten') house, it was actually built, of limestone with granite dressings, around 1498 by the successful merchant Thomas Yogge.

Turn left through the car park below Prysten House. Turn right up Catherine Street to visit St Andrew's church, Devon's largest medieval parish church with a 41m high tower. St Andrew's was substantially rebuilt after severe damage during the Blitz (as tableaux explain), gaining bold and colourful new stained glass windows. Turn left to the Guildhall Square, passing the Guildhall (16). From the Guildhall Square, cross Royal Parade into pedestrianised Armada Way.

The Drake's Circus shopping centre was opened in 2006 at a cost of £200 million

Walk up Armada Way to the 9m high stainless steel Sundial (17), with its fountain ringed by granite and metal seats highlighting countries of the world. Continue up Armada Way.

Take the next right (18), signed DRAKE'S CIRCUS, into pedestrianised CORNWALL STREET. The Drake's Circus shopping centre (19) at the top of Cornwall Street is a huge mall designed to update Plymouth's retail image and draw more trade into the city.

Follow Cornwall Street (no longer pedestrianised, so take care) round to the left, to a pedestrian crossing with traffic lights. Cross and turn right past the Roland Levinsky Building (20). Part of Plymouth University but open to the public, it has a restaurant, art gallery and programme of lectures, films, theatre and music.

Turn right across the road to visit the City Museum and Art Gallery (21), built in 1907 in a style described as 'Edwardian baroque'. The archaeology and history areas have a wealth of local exhibits and touch screen computers. The galleries include paintings by local artists such as Sir Joshua Reynolds, as well as Plymouth porcelain and Devon studio pottery.

Rebuilding Plymouth after the Blitz

Armada Way and Royal Parade are the major streets of Plymouth's post-war reconstruction. These broad thoroughfares were the vision of City Engineer James Paton-Watson and Sir Patrick Abercrombie, the architect who replanned several post-war cities, including London, Hull, Bath and Edinburgh. In adopting a bold modern plan they rejected the alternative of rebuilding central Plymouth's narrow and crowded pre-war streets.

Return to the roundabout and bear left down the dual carriageway, then cross to the opposite pavement. Follow the pavement around to the right at the next roundabout, Charles Cross, where the shell of 17th century Charles Church (22) stands as a memorial to Plymouth's Second World War civilian casualties.

Continue to St Andrew's Cross with its fountains. Keep right around the roundabout and cross ROYAL PARADE at the traffic lights by the church. Walk straight ahead, past the church on your right, down to the Plymouth Magistrates Court.

Turn left into HIGHER LANE and through controversially named Sir John Hawkins Square. Sir John Hawkins (1532-95) was born nearby, and as Treasurer of the Navy oversaw the development of the Elizabethan navy which defeated the Armada. He was a Vice Admiral in that battle – but he was also the first Englishman to become involved in the slave trade, in particular to the Caribbean.

Emerging from Higher Lane, turn right, noticing another ancient house (23) immediately on your right. Descend BUCKWELL STREET (once the High Street of Sutton Prior) and at the foot of the hill cross Notte Street, turn left and immediately right into BASKET OPE, then turn left and follow the right-hand side of the harbour, past outdoor eating places in front of converted warehouses, and turn right at the far end of the quay to return to Mayflower Steps.

BOAT TRIPS

Whilst the Hoe offers splendid views, there is no better way to see Plymouth Sound and appreciate the immense importance of the sea to Plymouth, and of Plymouth to the Navy, than by taking boat trips. Some are designed for tourists, but others are ferries which hold the city together in much the same way as the water-buses of Venice.

Mount Batten ferry

The Mount Batten ferry (01752 408590) gives great views of Sutton Harbour and the Citadel and runs year round from the Barbican to Turnchapel, a village of considerable character. To visit Turnchapel, disembark at the Mount Batten ferry pier, turn left and walk along the quay till you reach a road. Walk up the road for 60 m, then turn left, following the pedestrian route as signed, through the yacht haven.

Mount Batten Tower.

The tower and fort were named after William Batten. After assisting at the siege of Plymouth in 1644, Batten was appointed commander of the Parliamentary Navy in 1645. He later served Charles II as Surveyor of the Navy and was pilloried by Samuel Pepys in his diary for his bungling and corruption

Left: the village of Turnchapel

Drake's Island, previously known as St Nicholas's Island

The path passes between an apartment block and the marina. Follow SOUTH WEST COASTAL PATH TURNCHAPEL up steps to a car park. Turn left here, down a lane into Turnchapel.

A shorter walk from the ferry pier leads to Mount Batten Tower. From the pier, go through the park with its RAF memorial and straight up a lane. A path on the right leads to the tower. A superb viewpoint, it was probably built between 1646 and 1672 in conjunction with Plymouth Citadel to counter the Dutch naval threat.

Dockyards and Warships Cruise

Departing regularly from the Barbican landing stage, the 'Dockyards and Warships' cruise (01752 822105) has plenty of interest. The Citadel, Plymouth Hoe, Drake's Island and Mount Edgcumbe Country Park can all be seen from the boat and there is a more distant view of the Tamar Bridges. Devonport Dockyards, the most extensive in Western Europe, are hugely impressive – especially from the river.

Live commentary highlights points of interest on the cruise and in particular Royal Navy ships, the coming and going of which has been the staple of Plymouth news ever since the dockyards were first built in 1690. The hour-long cruise can be extended to a half or full day out by taking the option of disembarking at Mount Edgcumbe – a combined ticket covering the cruise with Mount Edgcumbe's house and garden is available.

The Cremyll Ferry on the Mount Edgcumbe side, with Stonehouse and the Royal William Yard in the background

Lower photo: Mount Edgcumbe. The house is furnished with family possessions, including paintings by Plympton-born Sir Joshua Reynolds, 16th century tapestries and porcelain from both China and Plymouth.

Mount Edgcumbe House and the adjoining Earl's Garden are open Sundays to Thursdays from April to September (admission charge, 01752 822236)

Cremyll Ferry and Mount Edgcumbe

A Grade 1 listed country park of 350 ha (865 acres), Mount Edgcumbe is open daily and free of charge all year. It's only seven minutes from Stonehouse by the Cremyll Ferry – a trip that takes you straight out of the city into the country, as well as giving splendid views of the Royal William Yard (below) and the Sound.

Edgcumbe has formal gardens, contrasting with woods full of wild-flowers, and a delightful camellia trail. Mount Edgcumbe House, the Earl's Garden and the Barrow Park Centre with its restored workshops are a ten minute walk from the ferry slipway. For the energetic, there are miles of footpaths to explore through the deer park, woods and fields or along the coast to the old smuggling villages of Cawsand and Kingsand – conveniently close for supplying Plymouth and even the ships of His Majesty's Navy with contraband!

In the Mount Edgcumbe Country Park, a large area of gardens and parkland is open to the public without charge.

The Orangery (right) very near the landing place of the Cremyll ferry, is open as a restaurant.

The formal gardens near the Orangery are in classical English, French and Italian styles, but more informal plantings are near at hand

Sir Richard Edgcumbe built Mount Edgcumbe as his main home in 1547-50, leaving the old family home at Cotehele (page 38) almost a time capsule. The Edgcumbes later developed the colourful gardens, with their orangery and elegant statues, complementing the park with its handsome avenues and specimen trees. Incendiary bombs gutted the house during the Blitz in 1941, but enough of the structure survived for it to be rebuilt. Don't miss the nearby Barrow Park Centre, which has a preserved sawmill and wheelwright's and blacksmith's workshops. A free film explains the long history of Mount Edgcumbe and special features in the park, such as the battery with its naval cannon next to the Formal Gardens. Bats roost in these buildings and can be watched on 'bat cam'.

The Cremyll Ferry runs all year, departing Admirals Hard, Stonehouse every 30 minutes. Signed car park. 01752 822105.

Royal William Yard

A dignified architectural gem in limestone and granite, Royal William Yard with its impressive entrance arch crowned with a statue of King William IV, is only a five minute walk from the Cremyll Ferry.

Alternatively, take a ferry directly to the Yard from the Barbican for an especially impressive view of it, as well as Drake's Island, the Hoe and Stonehouse Pool (hourly service, May to September, 01752 659252). There are two café/bars at the Yard and a gallery. At the time of writing, plans to move part of Devonport Naval Museum to the Yard were under way.

Boat trips further afield

Calstock: This four hour cruise from the Barbican takes the same route as the dockyard cruise, but continues past Saltash and under the Tamar Bridges.

Cawsand: The cruise from the Barbican around Rame Head to the old smuggling village of Cawsand is also a pleasure. Contact 01752 822105 for Calstock, 07833 936863 for Cawsand service.

MORE PLACES TO SEE

National Marine Aquarium

With its huge well lit glass-fronted tanks, the Aquarium brings visitors face to face with the marine environment and many species of fish. The Atlantic Reef Tank features fish from local waters; Caribbean species have another tank; whilst the Coral Seas Tank includes turtles and wonderfully coloured tropical fish. The Shallow Waters Area features local marine life and includes a shark hatchery. Run as a conservation charity, the Aquarium aims to raise public awareness of the fragile marine environment.

Saltram

Saltram is one of Devon's most impressive country houses and proved an ideal setting for the film *Sense and Sensibility* (1995), based on Jane Austen's novel and starring Emma Thompson and Kate Winslet. The core of the house is 16th century, but it was transformed in the 18th into an elegant mansion by the wealthy Parker family. Robert Adam designed the magnificent state rooms. The gardens are noted for their specimen trees, shrubberies and orangery. There is also an art gallery, summerhouse and garden temple to explore.

National Trust: 01752 333500. Location: 5km east of Plymouth city centre near Plympton.

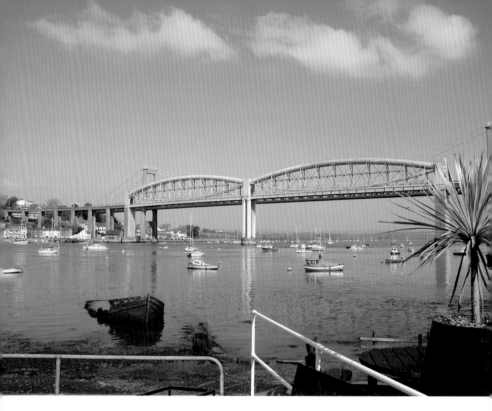

The Tamar Bridges

Although Plymouth was joined to Britain's burgeoning rail network in 1848, and Cornwall already had many railways , I K Brunel's railway bridge to Saltash was not completed until 1859, after six years' work.

The 667 m long bridge is one of Brunel's most enduring triumphs. He used bold and experimental engineering, including huge oval tubes to suspend the bridge and working at pressure below water level to build the piers. Wisely choosing corrosion-resistant wrought iron, Brunel built a bridge so strong it still carries today's (far heavier) mainline trains.

The neighbouring road bridge, which carries the A38 into Cornwall, was also bold and innovative. When completed in 1961, it was the longest suspension bridge in the UK. Before that, traffic had to use ferries or make the long detour north to Gunnislake to bridge the river Tamar. In 2001, it was the first suspension bridge in the world to be widened using cantilevers, which increased its capacity from three lanes to five: one new lane for cyclists and pedestrians, one for local traffic.

Antony House

EXCURSIONS

Antony

In Antony House film director Tim Burton found 'the perfect pocket sized mansion' for shooting key scenes in his *Alice in Wonderland* (2010). Anyone who has seen the film will readily recognise Antony and its delightful terraced gardens. These feature rhododendrons, azaleas, camellias and magnolias, whilst the parkland with its splendid trees and wildflowers stretches down to the river Lynher.

Antony House was built in Queen Anne style between 1711 and 1721 in silvery grey Pentewan stone for Sir William Carew, whose family had owned the estate since 1492: the Carew-Poles still live there.

National Trust: 01752 812191. Location 3 km west of Torpoint, reached via car ferry from Devonport.

Buckland Abbey

The home of Sir Francis Drake (page 7) Buckland Abbey is a curious mixture of medieval monastery and Elizabethan mansion. Begin by visiting the 14th century tithe barn; the most impressive monastic element, it shows the power of the medieval church in England. Nearly 50m long, it handled revenues in kind from the abbey's vast 8000 ha holdings. Outstanding among the Elizabethan elements is the Great Hall. Once the crossing of the abbey church, the Great Hall has a marvellous plaster ceiling, period furniture and a huge decorated fireplace dated 1576, all stating the power of its new secular owners. Also of interest are the Elizabethan gardens, craftsmen's workshops and walking trails.

National Trust: 01822 853706. Location: 17 km north of Plymouth near Buckland Monachorum.

Cotehele

This is one of Britain's least altered medieval country houses. The furniture and tapestries are especially appealing, as are the weaponry and armour – Cotehele was built of hard granite and slate with small high windows and strong doors to be easily defensible. The landscaped valley gardens overlook Calstock Viaduct and the river Tamar. In the grounds, criss-crossed with miles of footpaths, are a dovecote and an 18th century prospect tower.

Visitors can also see the Quay, with a medley of old buildings and a Tamar barge, as well as nearby Cotehele Watermill, with its preserved artisans' workshops.

National Trust: 01579 351346. Location: 22 km from Plymouth via Saltash Bridge.

Tamar Valley Railway

This 22 km branch railway through the Tamar Valley to Gunnislake is one of the most attractive in Britain and an extraordinary survival. From Plymouth's North Road station, the railway runs via Devonport and Keyham, giving a great view of the Dockyards.

It passes under the Tamar Bridges (another great view) to Bere Ferrers, where the station is preserved in period style, with a visitor

Opposite: Cotehele House (National Trust, entry fee), a superb late medieval house, with a variety of gardens

Top right: Calstock Quay, with a train crossing the viaduct

Right: The preserved barge 'Shamrock' at Cotehele Quay (free) – a reminder that the Tamar used to be an important commercial waterway

centre, vintage carriages and engines. It continues to Bere Alston then reverses to Calstock, once a busy Tamar port.

The railway passes 36m above the Tamar by the Calstock Viaduct to Calstock and Gunnislake. Take time to stop and explore these villages on foot or enjoy a country walk (free walks packs from Plymouth Tourist Information).

One option is a lovely 2.5 km (1 1/2 mile) signed walk from Calstock Quay to Cotehele Quay (free) and Cotehele House (see above).

For beer drinkers, there's the Tamar Valley Rail Ale Trail – with 18 pubs en route it's just as well you're not driving! National Rail Enquiries 08457 484950.

Useful information

Tourist Information Centre: Plymouth Mayflower,
3-5 The Barbican, 01752 306 330

Transport
Parking: There are 19 signed car parks in the city centre.
Park and ride (signed at Marsh Mills, Derriford and Milehouse,
Monday to Saturday) is much cheaper for all day parking.
National Rail Enquiries: 08457 48 49 50
Buses: Traveline on 0870 608 2 608

Places to visit
Merchant's House and Elizabethan House 01752 304771
National Marine Aquarium 0844 8937938
Royal William Yard 01752 659252
Plymouth Gin Distillery 01752 665292
Plymouth Museum and Art Gallery 01752 304774
Smeaton's Tower 01752 304774

Some other Bossiney Books for south Devon
Shortish Guide: Dartmouth
Shortish Guide: The South Hams

Really Short Walks South Devon
Shortish Walks South Devon Coast

The Devon Beach and Cove Guide
Devon's Geology: an introduction
Devon's History
Devon Place Names
Devon's Railways
Devon Smugglers: The truth behind the fiction
Sir Francis Drake: Devon's flawed hero

and for Dartmoor
Shortish Guide: High Dartmoor
Really Short Walks South Dartmoor
Shortish Walks on Dartmoor
Walks on High Dartmoor

For a full list, please see our website: www.bossineybooks.com